WANDER & WONDER
ഏ THE POETRY OF SCOTT OKI ൙

ISBN 97817374094-7-2
Library of Congress Control Number: 2023907703

First printing edition 2023 in the United States of America

o-kaisha Publishing
10838 Main Street | Suite 200
Bellevue, WA 98004

WANDER
&
WONDER

THE POETRY OF
SCOTT OKI

TABLE OF CONTENTS

TABLE OF CONTENTS
CONTINUED

INTRODUCTION

Writing poetry has become a source of peace and creativity for me—a ritual of meditation and exploration.

The cover art for "Wander & Wonder" features stacked stones called cairns, which symbolize being on the right path. One must trust those who placed them there and consider if their journey aligns with one's own.

The Cairn Series of poetry comprises a total of seven books which form a cairn of their own:

Chisana
Wabi-Sabi
Explorations
Wander & Wonder
Contemplations
Musings
Confluence

This series of stacked books also reflects my own journey, as explored through a wide variety of poetry; "Wander & Wonder" in particular navigates my own life experiences through the rhythmic form of lyrical poetry. I hope you enjoy this journey of discovery with me.

- Scott

Take a Walk

Take a slow stroll on the gentle side
With your new love tucked by your side
Savor soft kisses, squeeze each other tightly
As the breeze caresses oh so lightly

Don't pass by the ice cream vendor
Or you'll not indulge in his splendor
Treat your taste buds to an ice cream cone
Meant to be shared, not eaten alone

Capture the laughter and joyful smiles
In photographs that last for miles
Sip some beers, but don't overdo
Better the memory when kept to a few

Take lots of candid photographs
That create plenty of belly laughs
You might even take some videos
For much in life, anything goes

Take a weekend trip, just for two
And escape to a place brand new
It doesn't matter where you go
But hold hands, walk, and let love flow

Have you reached your daily goal
Strolling over knoll after knoll?
Fourteen thousand steps is a very long way
Especially so on a rainy, blustery day

Read books light and carefree
Indulge in moments of lip-sync glee
Close your eyes and dream again
Hold onto joy like a cherished gem

As you return to your humble abode
Let your heart overflow with love's load
Close your eyes and let sleep embrace
And then dream of life's deeper grace

Laurie

Bonding at first sight
Her eyes always so bright
You know it was meant to be
On that we could agree

So beautiful inside and out
There simply was no doubt
Lots of brown curly hair
Wafting in the summer air

She is extremely outgoing
Has others quickly glowing
A gift for inclusive conversations
Always lots of interesting questions

We have so much in common
Which is quite a phenomenon
Based on a foundation of love
Fitting each other like a glove

Embracing each other's family
Happily, affably, and sincerely
This is a critical two-way street
Absent this we would not be complete

We take care of each other
But together we don't smother
An occasional fight or two
Understanding the other's view

Communicating could be better
Less texting versus a note or letter
But I am an introvert
It's difficult to assert

We have so many things in common
Maybe it's a lucky phenomenon
Wanting a family to call our own
Not that bad if they're all clones

Raising babies was such a joy
Matters not whether girls or boys
A great education is key
Like the sturdy roots of a tree

Instilling life values is critical
Remember you can't be hypocritical
Also insert a healthy dose of fun
Outside, and ideally in the sun

Great family fun is travel
Wherever you go, revel
Exploring different cultures and food
Keeps the entire family glued

Laurie makes all the travel arrangements
I happily take care of all the payments
Hotels have to be nice and clean
A tiny bit of dust would be obscene

She's a voracious reader; I write
A pithy poem at a stoplight
I buy jewelry, she wears it
Fortunately it's often a hit

She is always hot, I am cold
Behold, I am also getting old
We both love our Sienna van
Kids and strollers is where that began

We care about those less fortunate
In fact, we are downright passionate
Emotions are central to a marriage
It's an institution you can't disparage

Laurie, I love you so much
I see stars at your touch
Especially the slightest touch of your lips
That's always something I cannot resist

Babies

A sight to behold, a miracle of life
A baby emerging amid all the strife
Head popping out of the womb
Adding to the world's joyful boom

A lifeline cut...the umbilical cord
But please, not with a samurai sword
With surgical scissors if you will
Your spine might still feel a chill

Momma suckling her newborn
On that precious early morn
Wishing it could last forever
A closeness you never want to sever

Impossible to avoid changing diapers
Now it's time to pay the pipers
Disposable ones are easily the best
Unless you're on an environmental quest

Don't you love it when they stare?
They do it with a magical flair
Their tiny hands with a power grip
Their version of gamesmanship

They'll let you know if something isn't right
A loud cry in the middle of the night
A nice warm cuddle is your reaction
For your baby's complete satisfaction

Can you be happier than when they smile
A smile much wider than a nautical mile
The quiet, contented sounds of cooing
It leads to your emotional undoing

They are your babies, forevermore
A love like no other, to your very core

Thoughts on Mom

What makes you so darned unique?
Must be your mothering technique
It started with taking care of three
   male siblings
So mothering was instilled from the
   early beginnings

     Mom, you are simply amazing
     We are all star gazing
     Twenty-six is the magic number to be
     Always older and wiser than me

Times were tough in the early years
But there were never many tears
It is hard for me to fathom the challenges
Living a modest life close to the fringes

     Mom, you are simply amazing
     We are all star gazing
     Twenty-six is the magic number to be
     Always older and wiser than me

Getting through high school was a breeze
Then came Pearl Harbor and a virtual freeze
Minidoka Idaho is no fairy tale land
Does not take close inspection to know it is
   extremely bland

Mom, you are simply amazing
We are all star gazing
Twenty-six is the magic number to be
Always older and wiser than me

With meager belongings to make a
  new home
We came together to avoid the
  homelessness syndrome
Summers so hot; winters so cold
Bringing your ice skates was very bold

Mom, you are simply amazing
We are all star gazing
Twenty-six is the magic number to be
Always older and wiser than me

Falling in love with Dad
For this we are all glad
Making it almost seventy years in marriage
And we know you did not have a
  marriage carriage

Mom, you are simply amazing
We are all star gazing
Twenty-six is the magic number to be
Always older and wiser than me

A short honeymoon to Utah
Even today, I remain in awe
Off to Japan in the army for Dad
While you mothered Mothers and your Dad

Mom, you are simply amazing
We are all star gazing
Twenty-six is the magic number to be
Always older and wiser than me

You gave birth to three babies
All without going crazy
Bouncing us on your knee
To our unfettered glee

Mom, you are simply amazing
We are all star gazing
Twenty-six is the magic number to be
Always older and wiser than me

Remember the drum corps days?
Always there to root and praise
So quietly strong and supportive
Never negative, always positive

Mom, you are simply amazing
We are all star gazing
Twenty-six is the magic number to be
Always older and wiser than me

Beginnings were tough but no complaining
Money challenges were always straining
Clipping coupons became a routine
The lean, mean, clipping machine

Mom, you are simply amazing
We are all star gazing
Twenty-six is the magic number to be
Always older and wiser than me

Now, five grandchildren, one great one
Did you ever imagine life so fun?
You are so darned easy to please
I would do anything to appease

Mom, you are simply amazing
We are all star gazing
Twenty-six is the magic number to be
Always older and wiser than me

Everyone loves you more than a flower
    bouquet
As your eldest son, I get to shout out
    and say:
You are my mother
And loved like no other

Happy One Hundred and One!!

Japan

Grandparents immigrated from Japan
Well before there was ever a ban
It's hard to imagine their courageousness
For them, they couldn't really reassess

They came from Hiroshima-ken
Not much on their backs and very little yen
They spoke Japanese but little English
But their excitement was not diminished

I have been to Japan 100 times
I slept on the plane sometimes
Then directly to meetings
Replete with formal greetings

Our first family trip with mom and dad
We were excited but it started off very sad
Uncle Katsumi died the day before
He stayed in Japan during, and after the war

Throughout Japan there is no litter
Things are always aglitter
Crime is virtually nonexistent
If it exists, it is very distant

There is no homelessness
Why not is anyone's guess
Everyone is so helpful and polite
Easily mistaken for an acolyte

Traveling on the bullet train
Almost as fast as an airplane
To stay at a ryokan in Kyoto
Memories captured in a photo

Communal baths with the boys
And no one lost their poise
Sleeping on a tatami mat
Very stiff and perfectly flat

Kyoto has lots of famous temples
That have withstood earthquake tremors
Nothing quite as beautiful as flowering
    cherry trees
Especially on a sunny day with a
    slight breeze

An origami master mesmerized
But then they do specialize
Folding objects in mid air
All the while with quite a flair

Lots of great powder skiing
Rental equipment not very freeing
The Nagano Games quite special
Even if Secret Service were the
    Tasmanian Devil

Wherever you are the food is all the rave
Be patient, wait in line, and behave
Restaurant specialization is the key
You will definitely gorge yourself with glee

Totemo oishikatta
Sayonara

Cycle of Life

How do caterpillars morph into butterflies?
Mother Nature provides the special ties
Their process is fast
But is it built to last?

> Everything in life transforms
> Conforming to certain norms

We go from babies to children
A wonderful time to bond with brethren
What is the size of your caste?
Does it matter if it's small or vast?

> Everything in life transforms
> Conforming to certain norms

Teenagers go through many stages
Puberty is just one of the phases
At times they may act like a clown
Eventually things do settle down

> Everything in life transforms
> Conforming to certain norms

Adulthood can span many decades
Although memory eventually fades
Love may come and go
Through it all they grow

> Everything in life transforms
> Conforming to certain norms

Eventually we become old folks
Sturdy and wise like old oaks
It's similar to being a sage
Telling stories as though on a stage

    Everything in life transforms
    Conforming to certain norms

Aging

As a septuagenarian, what's on my mind?
Anything I want if I'm so inclined
Hearing loss is real but fixable
Hearing aids are most viable

      Aging is inevitable
      Giving up is untenable

A sprint becomes a walk, then a ride
If you can, do the Michael Jackson glide
Loss of mobility is certainly real
You won't be doing a cartwheel

      Aging is inevitable
      Giving up is untenable

Osteoarthritis prevents simple things
Opening jars or tying shoestrings
Very painful playing golf or doing Gung Fu
Sadly, it's hard to even operate a corkscrew

      Aging is inevitable
      Giving up is untenable

Many reasons for memory loss
Perhaps ingesting too much secret sauce
Dementia is hard to deal with
That science can fix it all is a myth

      Aging is inevitable
      Giving up is untenable

What about the organ that all else relies on?
Without your heart, you are gone
Watch how much and what you eat
Better to have more veggies than meat

> Aging is inevitable
> Giving up is untenable

I believe aging can be slowed
Stimulate the brain and let neurons explode
Read, write poetry or your memoir
No one will think of it as bizarre

> Aging is inevitable
> Giving up is untenable

Pumping Iron

I weighed 115 pounds in college
Didn't go to class, didn't acquire knowledge
Met bodybuilder Pete Larson
He said, "Join me, it'll be fun"

We worked out at the Totem gym
Rats filled it almost to the brim
Pro wrestlers went there to train
Even with a leaky roof in the rain

Pete had me start light
After all, I was slight
Each lift had to be strict
Until it all clicked

For days I could not get out of bed
My few muscles were totally shred
Persevered and stuck to it
It would be too easy to quit

Quickly added 25 pounds of muscle
You would not want to tussle
Two-a-days were the norm
Had to maintain strict form

In six months, I could bench press
    280 pounds
With breathing and incoherent
    grunting sounds
Started doing two workouts each day
Not shy about my muscles on display

This was the start to a lifelong quest
To be able to puff up my chest
Many things complement pumping iron
Like making a roar like a lion!

At one time had 17.5-inch arms
Could probably work on a farm
Over the years my arms have lifted tons
Love my nickname: Scotty Guns!

Okay, it's time to do more cardio
Put headphones on and listen to the radio

Stay Trim

"Trim" is in the eye of the beholder
Some just shrug and give a cold shoulder
If you want to lose weight
Try the following list of eight

First, be regular about exercise
It doesn't count to stand and bake pies
Aerobic exercise is the best
Twenty minutes for your heart, then rest

Second, eat plenty of fiber that is soluble
With lots of water this is very valuable
Third, eat a high protein diet
This won't create a riot

Fourth, cut back on refined carbs
Or trade them for a deck of cards
Fifth, don't drink too much alcohol
Rule of moderation you must install

Sixth, avoid trans-fat foods
This will mean a change in attitude
Seventh, reduce stress levels
Do this before your life dishevels

Eighth, don't eat foods with sugar
It's not just de rigueur
I must stop eating M&M's
Impossible to give up on them

Is it worth the effort?!

Tattoos

I have had a big tattoo
Even had to wait in a queue
A henna tattoo at an Indian wedding
Took some time so could have been sleeping

In many cultures tattoos are not taboo
Especially so with needles of bamboo
They say this technique really hurts
For those who are pain averse

Dyes are inserted into the dermis layer of skin
This is performed with a very fine pin
Tattoos can be pictorial, symbolic,
    or decorative
If at all painful I'd be screaming expletives

The Yakuza in Japan wear a full body suit
Very terrorizing and not very cute
Oldest tattoo found on Otzi the Iceman
    in 3250 BC
Archeologists jumped with unfettered glee

14% of Americans have one
Many choose to have tattoos undone
Annually $1.6 Billion is spent
That's a whole lot of cents

More women than men have them
Some can be real gems
Women are twice as likely to have
them removed
So, what exactly does that prove?

Fun

You can have lots of fun alone
Even if you are full grown
Learn a new skill
Might give you a thrill

      Fun is definitely not one and done
      Adopt the attitude, we've only
        just begun

I'm learning to play the ukulele soprano
In Hawaiian not a mano
Relearning to play the clarinet
Alternate fingerings I did forget

      Fun is definitely not one and done
      Adopt the attitude, we've only
        just begun

Clean out that cluttered closet
Might find a certificate of deposit
Enough to buy a new car
Now that would be bizarre

      Fun is definitely not one and done
      Adopt the attitude, we've only
        just begun

Take that new car and wash it
Work and no fun, then quit
Might require some TLC
Matters not a he or she

    Fun is definitely not one and done
    Adopt the attitude, we've only
      just begun

Breakdance to raise money
Make kids' lives a bit more sunny
Or just breakdance any ol' time
Even if you are past your prime

    Fun is definitely not one and done
    Adopt the attitude, we've only
      just begun

Spam musubi with mom
She is always so calm
But this brings a smile
Wider than a mile

    Fun is definitely not one and done
    Adopt the attitude, we've only
      just begun

Work

Nothing but work and zero play...
Might not lead to a satisfying day
But the harder you work the luckier you get
It's okay to break out in a sweet sweat

> Work smart but also have some fun
> Tomorrow's soon enough begun

When you are working, have a
  maniacal ethic
I would never consider that to be pathetic
Entrepreneurial endeavors mandate this
If it's absent, may not reach success

> Work smart but also have some fun
> Tomorrow's soon enough begun

Everyone should have a startup experience
Outcomes may have a large variance
But you will learn many life lessons
They will leave indelible impressions

> Work smart but also have some fun
> Tomorrow's soon enough begun

You will acquire lots of scar tissue
For the future this is not an issue
Matters not failure or success
For the opportunity feel blessed

Work smart but also have some fun
Tomorrow's soon enough begun

What is your long-term passion?
Could range from high tech to fashion
Regardless of what it is, work smart
This is what will set you apart

Work smart but also have some fun
Tomorrow's soon enough begun

You form many close relationships
For those consider yourself blessed
But business is second to home
Open up a favorite jeroboam

Work smart but also have some fun
Tomorrow's soon enough begun

Not possible to make more time
Work until you hear the alarm chime
Use twenty-four hours wisely
You'll be rewarded quite nicely

Work smart but also have some fun
Tomorrow's soon enough begun

Balance work with health, friends,
    and family
Do this and avoid a calamity
Be honest in your assessment
Don't place yourself in a predicament

     Work smart but also have some fun
     Tomorrow's soon enough begun

Dream

I dream that no one goes hungry
Here or any other country
Hunger leaves an indelible mark
Leaves humans looking very stark

    Sit me by a river or stream
    To contemplate and live my dream

Every child needs a great education
Building toward a better nation
Arm them with these lifelong tools
They'll be brightly shining jewels

    Sit me by a river or stream
    To contemplate and live my dream

Make peace with mother nature
Slow the melting of a glacier
Stop unnecessary deforestation
Might require strict legislation

    Sit me by a river or stream
    To contemplate and live my dream

Stop exploiting child labor
No way is this good behavior
Put their minds at work in schools
Here they will learn the power of rules

Sit me by a river or stream
To contemplate and live my dream

Heal all of the geopolitical rifts
Please don't give this short shrift
There is nothing pleasant about war
It's just plain wrong...always lots of gore

Sit me by a river or stream

**To contemplate and live
my dream.**

Travel

So many places to visit
Sit, gaze, ask, "What is it?"

Antarctica is at the top of my list
The only continent I have missed
An ecosystem pristine and severe
The largest desert, no water here

What is there in Iceland?
Lots...go there to understand
Bathe in the Blue Lagoon
Start in the morning, stay 'til noon

I will never tire of Africa
Going on foot requires stamina
There is wildlife galore
Might even adore the roar

Egypt is famous for its great pyramids
Framed by the sun, it's hard to close
   your eyelids
Also known as tetrahedrons
Still discovering many salons

Visit the Tokaji vineyards
Essential for diehards
Also indulge in Hungarian coffee
Drink it with the delicious toffee

Machu Picchu is a must-see place
High elevations with a misty grace
You will be in awe of the ruins
They were actually built by humans

Go visit the Great Barrier Reef
But global warming is giving it grief
Largest living thing on earth
Please give it a wide berth

Victoria Falls is the largest
Painted by many artists
The Falls create "moon bows"
It is a lunar rainbow

So many places to visit
Sit, gaze, ask, "What is it?"

Pioneers

The Venetian explorer Marco Polo
Leadership was somewhat solo
Extensive travel to Asia
China not Micronesia

Christopher Columbus
Did he use a compass?
Nina, Pinta and Santa Maria
The Age of Discovery

They brought animals and food
This was on the whole good
But they also brought disease
Put lots of natives on their knees

Explorers Lewis and Clark
Certainly left their mark
Got along with our First Nations
Treated them like real civilians

They discovered the Pacific Northwest
This land is some of the very best
We've seen many changes over time
But land and maritime remain sublime

Sir Isaac Newton's famous discoveries
Most are baked into our memories
Every action has an equal reaction
On this there cannot be any abstraction

Martin Luther King and civil rights
Brought color differences into the light
"I have a dream" was the rallying cry
Many years later, it still applies

Grace Hopper left a big imprint on tech
Please don't say "what the heck"
Invented the first language compiler
"Grandma COBOL," geeks style her

Stephanie Kwolek invented Kevlar
Changing many things forever
Five times stronger than steel
This has broad appeal

Keep on truckin'

Greetings

Greetings, my friend
May our friendship never end

A heartfelt hello or hi
Better than goodbye
Hello is absolutely fine
Especially with a glass of wine

G'day mate
With the right accent, really great
How hops it
Takes a little wit

A simple handshake
No one will think of you a flake
If they are of a secret nature
A special nomenclature?

High fives are popular
Among those who are jocular
Fist bumps are the rage
Did this come from the ice age?

Palm grasp, hand slide, low five
Requires more than a bit of jive
But it is all so fun
Can never be just one and done

Bowing seems more formal
But in many cultures very normal
Deep respect is shown by a low bow
Uninitiated might say "wow"

The ultimate is a kiss on both cheeks
It might sweep you off your feet
But does the right or left cheek come first
Does it really matter if the order is reversed?

Greetings, my friend
May our friendship never end

Airport Codes

Ever wonder how they came about?
Not because they're easy to shout
They're three-letter acronyms
All unique, no synonyms

Started in the 1930's
First they were two-letter series
A decade later airports grew
And two letters were just too few

A shift to codes of letters three
Some are clear, some cheeky
ATL is for Atlanta
EEK is an airport in Alaska

Some codes are fun to tell
Nevada's Derby Field is LOL
PEE for Russia, POO is Brazil
Always give me quite a thrill

Those are just to name a few
How funny, I wonder if they knew
Is there a censor who oversees
Can I choose my own code, pretty please?

Palace on Wheels

Something magical about trains
A nice steady pace across Great Plains
The rocking back and forth
Any direction including magnetic north

       Love the rhythmic clickety clack
       So mesmerizing, you'll be back

The Palace on Wheels
Lots of appeal including the meals
Taking eight days to traverse India
Don't worry it won't head to Siberia

       Love the rhythmic clickety clack
       So mesmerizing, you'll be back

Plenty of sights from Rajasthan to Agra
Faster than saying abracadabra
Thirteen deluxe cars that transport you
Each has an attendant that sticks like glue

       Love the rhythmic clickety clack
       So mesmerizing, you'll be back

The trip starts in New Delhi
The welcoming garland is quite nice really
All aboard to dinner en route
Great meal with tea that was quite stout

Love the rhythmic clickety clack
So mesmerizing, you'll be back

Day two in Jaipur, the Pink City
Lots of homeless and a bit gritty
There is a memorable elephant ride
The road was steep and not very wide

Love the rhythmic clickety clack
So mesmerizing, you'll be back

Find yourself in the Ranthambore Tiger
    Reserve on day three
Get careless and you might end up
    an amputee!
Day four is in Udaipur, the City of Lakes
Boat to Palace Hotel for a break

Love the rhythmic clickety clack
So mesmerizing, you'll be back

Day five you are in Jaisalmer, Oasis in
    the Desert
It's not that hot so no need to take off
    your shirt
Jaisalmer Fort is right out of a fable
This tagline is a great label

Love the rhythmic clickety clack
So mesmerizing, you'll be back

Day six finds you in Jodhpur, Heart
  of Marwar
16th century forts like Mehrangart were
  built for war
Day seven you're in the Bhatarpur
  Bird Sanctuary
375 species of local and migratory birds but
  no apiary

> Love the rhythmic clickety clack
> So mesmerizing, you'll be back

Visit Agra and the Taj Mahal
It is the opposite of small
One of the 7 wonders of the modern world
Up close its white marble is whorled

> Love the rhythmic clickety clack
> So mesmerizing, you'll be back

Day eight is the end of the journey
Not so sure I'm glad you returned me
You've reached New Delhi
Go freely...but,

> Love the rhythmic clickety clack
> So mesmerizing, you'll be back

Thailand

A once-in-a-lifetime trip
One that sealed our courtship
In other words, our honeymoon
It would be over way too soon

Staying at the Peninsula Hotel
Soon had us under its spell
Bangkok is a fascinating city
Equal parts gritty and pretty

There were taxis galore
There wasn't a single door
Water taxis were really cool
A skillful dodging of whirlpools

Exploring all the back canals
Strangely lifting my morale
Real life revealed in early morning
Without preamble or forewarning

Then on to Phuket Island
Palm trees, sun, and lots of sand
Amanpuri Hotel was exquisite
Definitely earning a revisit

Only left the pool to eat
Our world there was quite complete
Two amazing restaurants
Every meal was worth a flaunt

Daily Scrabble at the pool
All we needed to be content and cool
Alas came the time to check out
It was difficult not to pout

Paris

Paris with the boys for six weeks
The fall air creating pink cheeks
French-American school was great
Having much fun is no debate

Walking from here to there
Fall was in the air
Taking the Métro sped things up
Taking a taxi was a runner-up

Callan was in Laurie's tummy
Waiting to make her a mommy
Jambon-beurre sandwiches
Cravings in two languages

Food and wine galore
It truly did restore
Duck confit an all-time favorite
Try to eat slowly so you can savor it

Museums of fine art
Do they allow a shopping cart?
Alas, time to say goodbye
With a tear in the eye

Au revoir

Serengeti

Visiting the Serengeti twice
Thrice would be very nice
Seeing the wildlife in open air Jeeps
Avoid animals that can leap

You get very close to animals of prey
Avoid being their meal for that day
The circle of life before your eyes
For some it is their demise

Wildlife everywhere you can see
Even during afternoon tea
Early morning hot air balloon
Sunrise, silence, then lunch at noon

Seventy large mammals call the
   Serengeti home
No fences anywhere and so they freely roam
Add in five hundred bird species
Only downside—their falling feces

The migration of Wildebeest a sight
   to behold
Two million gnus and zebra, all told
A fascinating symbiotic relationship
That does not involve a courtship

They migrate to follow the rains
Crossing many rivers and plains
From the Serengeti to Masai Mara
Where they eventually say *sayonara*

An eight hundred-kilometer trek
For everyone else a pain in the neck
Largest animal migration on the planet
Since the Almighty began it

So many animals to see
Keep quiet else they flee
You can get quite close
You are totally engrossed

All kinds of antelope
But they cannot marry or elope
Elands, Impalas, Gazelles
The latter are the belles

Springbok antelopes everywhere
Leaping from here to there
Antelope of many types
Some plain, some with stripes

Giraffes are Zaar's fave
Since childhood all the rave
Hippos and crocs wallow next to each other
Respect for a fellow water-bound brother

We witnessed a lion eating its prey
Its guts were very much on display
Lots of blood on the lion's face
He did not eat with much grace

A cache of hyenas would await
Occasionally they would aggravate
Eventually the lion would be done
The leftovers would be pounced upon

Where there are hyenas, there are vultures
Inbred with their own culture
They picked at what the hyenas left behind
Pecking order was well defined

Ostriches are so big they can't fly
But, they run and are very spry
Kori bustard is huge and can fly
The downdraft can keep you dry

A bunny teasing a leopard was quite a sight
It had no chance of putting up a fight
The leopard would pounce
The bunny would bounce

Lion prides can be quite large
The dominant male is in charge
Eats, fornicates and plays
Then climbs in a tree and just lays

I can never tire of the wonders
of the Serengeti...

Hawai'i

Hawai'i is so fascinatingly diverse
Many islands to traverse
More than just the major eight
Make up our western and southernmost state

> The state fish is the Reef Triggerfish
> Humuhumunukunukuapua'a

There are 137 different islands
Like a string of diamonds
Stretching 1,500 miles
Bringing lots of smiles

> The state fish is the Reef Triggerfish
> Humuhumunukunukuapua'a

Hawai'i is unique in so many ways
Each Big Eight island has a different lei
Leis can be made from different materials
Historically worn by the imperials

> The state fish is the Reef Triggerfish
> Humuhumunukunukuapua'a

Flowers, seashells, or nuts are
Leaves also but no cigar
Feathers, bones, animal teeth are okay
Wear leis there and away

> The state fish is the Reef Triggerfish
> Humuhumunukunukuapua'a

Hawai'i exclusively has public beaches
For surfers this is sweeter than peaches
Surfing was invented here
Ride some waves then quaff a beer

> The state fish is the Reef Triggerfish
> Humuhumunukunukuapua'a

Maui's Haleakala is the largest dormant
  volcano
Not sure how to say in Hawaiian so
  muy bueno
From the ocean floor, rises 33,500 feet
This simply cannot be beat

> The state fish is the Reef Triggerfish
> Humuhumunukunukuapua'a

Nearly a mile taller than Everest
It is temperate and maybe the best
Mauna Loa is the world's largest
  active volcano
So hot you'll have to walk away though

> The state fish is the Reef Triggerfish
> Humuhumunukunukuapua'a

Hawai'i is the only state with two official
 languages
Which is used in rough interchanges
Only 12 letters in the Hawaiian alphabet
So, learning it should be no sweat

 The state fish is the Reef Triggerfish
 Humuhumunukunukuapua'a

Underwater

Underwater sensation of weightlessness
So cool, you think you've been blessed
With it, comes peacefulness and tranquility
Audacious thought, there might be
  a calamity

With SCUBA, breathing is like taking
  your first
Warning: Do not do this unrehearsed
Comfort comes with a whole lot of practice
To get that feeling of floating on a mattress

Snorkeling allows observing what's below
If a mild current just go with the flow
The snorkel was invented by Leonardo
  da Vinci
If I'm dreamin' then pinch me

Is swimming that tranquil?
Even if not, we can still be thankful
Seems very aerobic to me
Nevertheless there's lots to see

Depending on where, lots of fish
So many it may fulfill a long-held wish
Coral reefs in all their splendor
Protect them; be their defender

Sea

The sea can be stormy or calm
If not too stormy, it can act like a balm
Stroll with sand between your toes
Washing away all your woes

> You and me
> We can be one with the sea

Braving the rough waves
Explore some sand caves
No telling what you might find
Sea turtles wanting to unwind

> You and me
> We can be one with the sea

Reflecting the rays of the sun
End the day with leisurely fun
Hand-in-hand to your favorite eating place
Don't gobble but eat with grace

> You and me
> We can be one with the sea

Embracing the sea even in the rain
If unprepared, it can be a pain
The beauty of the sea
Take it all in with glee

> You and me
> We can be one with the sea

Rain

At times rain can be a real pain
Without it crops are under strain
It has lifesaving properties too
Animals certainly don't eschew

  Rain, rain, come back soon
  Though I shrivel like a prune

Rainfall is the source of water
Absent, air dries and sun feels hotter
Access to water sustains life
Helps avoid any strife

  Rain, rain, come back soon
  Though I shrivel like a prune

Sometimes when it rains, it pours
You might want to batten down the doors
Floods may be on the way
Lay out the sandbags and pray

  Rain, rain, come back soon
  Though I shrivel like a prune

Heavy rains are why Wildebeest migrate
The Masai Mara is their heavenly gate
Over one million in orderly fashion
The crocs show no compassion

Rain, rain, come back soon
Though I shrivel like a prune

Instead of downpours, I like rain
  in sprinkles
Stay out long enough it might
  cause wrinkles
Rather lovely and who knows
You might see one or two rainbows

Rain, rain, come back soon
Though I shrivel like a prune

Ecology

Species variability
Is critical to sustainability
Disturbing self-organized balance
May possibly lead to a bad stance

      Ecological diversity
      Should not be a mystery

Human interaction threatens life
Many species under strife
Serious risk of survival
In other words, no revival

      Ecological diversity
      Should not be a mystery

Caribbean coral reefs
Once gone, tremendous grief
A natural barrier protecting the coast
Don't let the reefs become a ghost

      Ecological diversity
      Should not be a mystery

The Alaskan kelp forests
Absorbing carbon dioxide, one of the best
Home for many fish stocks
But, pollution spills are a real shock

Ecological diversity
Should not be a mystery

Murray-Darling basin wetlands
How long until it turns to sand?
Now at eighteen percent capacity
Accept an invitation to fix with alacrity

Ecological diversity
Should not be a mystery

Is global warming to blame?
Perhaps it's forest fire flames
Makes for an easy scapegoat
No place to run so get in your rowboat

Ecological diversity
We can fix it; you and me

Mushrooms

There's fungus among us
3.8 million species, some pileus
No one knows the exact number
What kind do you prefer?

      Mushrooms can be a boon to life
      Although a few may cause some strife

Shrooms can be eaten
But you might become a cretin
Stick with morels
You can rest on your laurels

      Mushrooms can be a boon to life
      Although a few may cause some strife

There are psychedelic properties
Making you a subspecies
Might be seeing all kinds of colors
Won't make you a scholar

      Mushrooms can be a boon to life
      Although a few may cause some strife

Certain fungi break down plastic
A much-needed feat of magic
Hiding unknown traits
No longer up for debate

Mushrooms can be a boon to life
Although a few may cause some strife

Toadstools remove toxins from oil spills
Nature's answer: no frills, no bills
Known to break down radioactive material
Hard to believe and most ethereal

Mushrooms can be a boon to life
Although a few may cause some strife

They are a source of antibiotics
Relationships can be symbiotic
So don't dismiss their potential
Might be existential

Mushrooms can be a boon to life
Although a few may cause some strife

Trees

Kahlil Gibran: "trees are poems"

Tens of thousands of tree species
Nurture them with kindness please
They can live for a long time
Some are very hard to climb

Methuselah is a Bristlecone pine
Looks very gnarly yet divine
Nearly 5,000 years old
A long time out in the hot and cold

The Monkey Puzzle tree
Children look at them with glee
They can live for 1,000 years
Almost bizarre so they appear

The Cypress Umbrella
Is one beautiful fella
Especially viewed from the island of Capri
Brings out the emotion of glee

The largest tree is named General Sherman
A giant sequoia that thwarts all vermin
The largest tree in the world
Its bark is beautifully burled

Maple trees produce 20 to 40 gallons of sap
Sap runs slow so you can take a nap
Squirrels also love the taste
Hard to stop them even when chased

Aspen trees are the largest single organism
    on earth
Give them a wide berth
Connected by their roots
A unique attribute

2,500 species of palms
Producing everything from fruits to alms
The Coco De Mer Palm produces
    66-point seeds
A wee too big for prayer beads

Can't forget the Papaya
We all love this even the Messiah
The sugar in Papaya produces energy
Just the opposite of lethargy

Kahlil Gibran: "trees are poems"

Moon

Man in the moon or on the moon
Both are sights to make us swoon
From ballads to odes and so much more
The moon's been sung for evermore

> Give me a full moon over a new one
> One is full of light, the other
>   displays none

Crescent moons keep changing shape
Sometimes in the form of a crepe
Moons that are full disappear too soon
Especially in the middle of a typhoon

> Give me a full moon over a new one
> One is full of light, the other
>   displays none

Our moon, our closest celestial friend
Mentioned by poets to no end
And when the sun and moon are seen
A juxtapositional pleasure exciting
   and serene

> Give me a full moon over a new one
> One is full of light, the other
>   displays none

Will there be permanent colonies
I think yes with no apologies
The views would be magnificent
And certainly very different

> Give me a full moon over a new one
> One is full of light, the other
>   displays none

Some singers croon to the moon
After too many drinks in a saloon
Imbibing in the evening or afternoon
It just doesn't matter if you sing in tune

> Give me a full moon over a new one
> One is full of light, the other
>   displays none

Moon colors, oh how they change,
From white to yellow and the strange
But blue, ah blue, my favorite hue
A calming sight that's oh so true

> Give me a full moon over a new one
> One is full of light, the other
>   displays none

Wonders of Nature

The Northern Lights
Oh, what a sight
Constantly changing colors
Makes you cry and holler

       The wonders of nature are endless
       Were they put there to impress?

The Grand Canyon National Park
So vast you might find a fossilized shark
Its ever changing contours
Provides a host to many tours

       The wonders of nature are endless
       Were they put there to impress?

Paricutin volcano in Mexico
Es muy joven y muy bueno
Able to fully document its birth
Still growing to change the earth

       The wonders of nature are endless
       Were they put there to impress?

The highest point is Everest
If you are going to summit, don't rest
It is quite the daunting test
You can take pride in the quest

The wonders of nature are endless
Were they put there to impress?

Rio de Janiero
The Harbour *es primero*
Boat traffic galore
Places to explore

The wonders of nature are endless
Were they put there to impress?

Victoria Falls and Zambezi River
Water is a life giver
Largest curtain of water
Makes a large imprimatur

The wonders of nature are endless
Were they put there to impress?

Great Barrier Reef is full of coral
Underwater they appear floral
Offering protection to many tiny fish
Or for octopi who can squish

The wonders of nature are endless
Were they put there to impress?

ACKNOWLEDGEMENTS

I would like to thank all the poets who have written various kinds of poetry since the 23rd Century BC Sumerian, Enheduanna. Since then, there have been many other famous poets. If it weren't for her, we might not have Michelangelo, Shakespeare, Ralph Waldo Emerson, Robert Frost, Walt Whitman, and many others writing in different poetic styles. Rhymed verse, acrostic poems, sonnets, haiku, ballads, limericks, and the extremely difficult-to-write villanelle among many others. In many ways I am indebted to their wonderful works and inspiration.

I would like to thank everyone involved in selecting the lyric poems embodied in Wander & Wonder. They helped me choose from a list of 105 lyric poems that I have written to date. We simply did not have enough room to put it all into this small form factor. Thanks to Susie Sharp and Nancy Cho and the GIRVIN team for all they do behind the scenes!

COLOPHON

This book was designed in collaboration with Scott Oki and the design team of GIRVIN, located in Seattle. The interior layout makes use of the geometry of the golden section, a secret canon which underlies many late medieval manuscripts, discovered by Jan Tschichold in 1953. The typeface used in this book, Georgia, was designed by Matthew Carter in 1993. The paper stock is Cougar Opaque Smooth.